TRACK & FIELD

Conditioning for Greatness

PREPARING FOR GAME DAY

BASEBALL & SOFTBALL: SUCCESS ON THE DIAMOND

BASKETBALL: STRATEGY ON THE HARDWOOD

CHEERLEADING: TECHNIQUES FOR PERFORMING

EXTREME SPORTS: POINTERS FOR PUSHING THE LIMITS

FOOTBALL: TOUGHNESS ON THE GRIDIRON

LACROSSE: FACING OFF ON THE FIELD

SOCCER: BREAKING AWAY ON THE PITCH

TRACK & FIELD: CONDITIONING FOR GREATNESS

VOLLEYBALL: APPROACHING THE NET

WRESTLING: CONTENDING ON THE MAT

PREPARING FOR GAME DAY

TRACK & FIELD
Conditioning for Greatness

Peter Douglas

MASON CREST

Mason Crest
450 Parkway Drive, Suite D
Broomall, Pennsylvania 19008
(866) MCP-BOOK (toll free)

First printing
9 8 7 6 5 4 3 2 1

ISBN (hardback) 978-1-4222-3920-9
ISBN (series) 978-1-4222-3912-4
ISBN (ebook) 978-1-4222-7875-8

Cataloging-in-Publication Data on file with the Library of Congress

QR CODES AND LINKS TO THIRD-PARTY CONTENT

CONTENTS

KEY ICONS TO LOOK FOR:

Words to understand: These words with their easy-to-understand definitions will increase the reader's understanding of the text while building vocabulary skills.

Sidebars: This boxed material within the main text allows readers to build knowledge, gain insights, explore possibilities, and broaden their perspectives by weaving together additional information to provide realistic and holistic perspectives.

Educational Videos: Readers can view videos by scanning our QR codes, providing them with additional educational content to supplement the text. Examples include news coverage, moments in history, speeches, iconic sports moments and much more!

Text-dependent questions: These questions send the reader back to the text for more careful attention to the evidence presented there.

Research projects: Readers are pointed toward areas of further inquiry connected to each chapter. Suggestions are provided for projects that encourage deeper research and analysis.

Series glossary of key terms: This back-of-the book glossary contains terminology used throughout this series. Words found here increase the reader's ability to read and comprehend higher-level books and articles in this field.

 ## WORDS TO UNDERSTAND:

adductor: a muscle that draws a body part toward the median line or toward the axis of an extremity

adverse: unfavorable or antagonistic in purpose or effect

toxins: poisonous substances that are specific products of the metabolic activities of a living organism and are usually very unstable

Chapter 1

MEET DAY

Track and field is a discipline that is made up of dozens of different events, from the 100 meter sprint and the marathon to the high jump and the javelin. Given the vast variety of these events, the preparation on the day of the meet can be quite different for the athletes as well.

In track and field, there are three basic types of events: running, jumping, and throwing. This chapter will discuss the differences, and the similarities, in preparation techniques for athletes in each type of event.

Whether you are a sprinter or a distance runner, jumper, or thrower, it is helpful to get some sleep the night before a race or event. Experts recommend a full eight hours, if possible. But even if nerves keep you up, or you cannot get as much sleep as would be ideal, do not let it bother you. Research indicates that if you have been sleeping well and regularly during training, one poor night of sleep should not have an **adverse** effect.

RUNNING

What to Wear

For sprinters, what to wear is pretty easy. No matter the temperature, sprinters should wear what they are used to racing in. In cold

> "You don't want to approach the long jump approach as if you're lowering yourself and then jumping. You want to keep your center of mass as high as possible so you can use all the momentum that you've built up for the entire run so you can get the most out of your jump."
>
> — Dwight Phillips,
> 2004 Olympic gold medalist

Preparation for runners is different than for athletes in jumping and throwing events.

weather, they can switch to heavier warm-up clothes and keep them on longer before it is time to race. For distance runners, this is a little trickier. As a general rule, runners should dress as if it is fifteen degrees warmer than the actual temperature. This will compensate for the natural heating of your body during the race. Prepare everything you plan to wear or take with you to the race before you go to sleep. This will give you one less thing to think about on race day.

What to Eat

Let's discuss distance running first. On the day of the race, you do not want to give your body too many calories to process that might detract from its primary task of running the race. You have already prepared your body by eating a big, carbohydrate-rich lunch the previous day, followed by a lighter but still high-carb dinner. On race day, ideally your breakfast should be no later than about five hours before the race starts. A 750-calorie fruit smoothie, for example, would be a good breakfast. Be sure to choose something very light. In the hours before the race, concentrate on remaining hydrated, alternating water with an electrolyte-rich drink. About an hour before the start, eat a protein bar and an energy gel with glycogen. Glycogen is your body's primary source of carbs and provides the energy

1984 Olympic marathon champion Joan Benoit Samuelson

needed to burn fat. You want your stomach to be mostly empty when the race starts. All the fuel you need is already in your system ready to be burned.

For sprinters, carb loading for races is not necessary. Their energy output is high, but fast, on race day. Therefore they should eat differently than they would for high-intensity training sessions that last for several hours. Race-day food choices should be low in fat and calories. What to eat depends on what time of day the race will occur. If the race will be at least four hours post-meal, then the meal should be hearty. Example meals include a turkey sandwich on wheat, brown rice with chicken, or whole grain pasta with sauce, not butter. Breakfast choices could include cereal with banana in low-fat milk or some fruit salad with low-fat yogurt.

For earlier races, between one and two hours before the race, the meal should be lighter. A fruit smoothie, low-fat yogurt, fruit, protein, or cereal bars and whole grain cereal in low-fat milk are all good options. About thirty minutes before the start, drink between six and twelve ounces of water.

Warm-Up
It is important for distance runners to try to keep their bodies warm and loose on race day. About three hours prior to race time, a runner should get in a light half-mile jog.

"Focus on this in training. Do not let your shoulders come up (when running), do not panic, keep the rhythm, and when they move and react, you move and react."

– Khadevis Robinson, four-time U.S. 800 meter outdoor champion

"You never know how you're going to feel on race days, so the best laid plans can sometimes go amok. So don't put too much emphasis into your race strategy because the day could come up totally differently from what you were expecting. Run the way you feel."

– Joan Benoit Samuelson, 1984 Olympic marathon gold medalist

About an hour before the race, another light jog at a pace half as fast as race speed for twenty-five minutes, surging eight times for twenty seconds at a time in the last mile, will get the heart pumping. The jog should be followed by warm-up drills:

- 20 rotational leg swings per leg: swing each leg from the hip from front to back and side to side.

- 60 standing toe raises per leg: stand with feet eight inches apart. Shifting your weight to the left foot, put the right foot a few inches ahead and raise your toes until you feel a stretch in the calf. Repeat with the left leg.

- 30 lateral steps: stand with feet shoulder width apart. Bend the knees, and crouch about six inches, leaning forward slightly. Keeping the body still, step to the side with the left leg as far as it will extend. Repeat on the right side.

- 40 high knees: from a standing position, quickly run in place, focusing on driving the knees toward the chin.

- 40 butt kicks: from a standing position, quickly run in place, focusing on bringing the heel to the buttocks with each step.

- 3 sets of four 20-second sprints (drink water in between as needed).

"It's always a good idea to plan out for the season ahead your targets and your goals that you really want to aim for."

– Paula Radcliffe, 2005 marathon world champion

It is always better to be a little too warm than to not be warm enough.

For the sprinters, the warm-up can consist of seven minutes of light jogging, followed by three to four minutes of butt kicks and high knees. The next step is five minutes of short (50 meter) sprints at race speed. The last fifteen minutes before the race should be spent stretching and getting ready to run.

After the race, cooling down is important as well. Spend five to ten minutes jogging lightly and then stretching immediately following the race. This will help to flush **toxins** that have built up in the muscles, which aids in recovery.

JUMPING

The jumping events include the field events of long jump, high jump, triple jump, and pole vault. With the exception of the high jump, they involve a sprinting element that leads up to the jump as well.

What to Wear

Athletes in the jumping event should dress according to the weather conditions, keeping in mind that they spend a lot of time during the event waiting between attempts. They should bring and wear easily removable sweats over their uniforms that will keep them warm in between.

Getting the proper rest helps athletes like world record holder in the pole vault Renaud Lavillenie of France perform at his best.

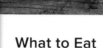

Eating complex, multigrain carbohydrates like bread and pasta is a good source of fuel for track-and-field athletes on meet days.

"You want to hit the ground and drive the thigh. As you get better at it, you'll notice that you're hitting the ground more actively and getting a better thigh drive, and that's always excellent. For running, for bounding, for jumping, it's the best technique that you can have."

– Willie Banks, three-time Olympic triple jumper

What to Eat

As is the case in the sprinting events, carb loading is not necessary for jumping events. Calories should be balanced among protein, fat, and carbohydrates. The last full meal should be eaten between three and four hours prior to competition. A lean-meat sandwich (e.g., turkey on whole grain bread) with fruit, beans, and nuts is an example of a good meal option. This should be accompanied by sixteen to twenty ounces of water or low-fat milk. About an hour before competing, a small snack like a low-fat granola bar is a good idea, along with another eight ounces of water. During the competition itself, athletes should focus on staying hydrated. Fluid intake will vary based on weather conditions as more will be required on hot days. In general, athletes should drink about eighteen ounces an hour. In weather where sweating is profuse, this should be augmented with eight ounces of a low-calorie sports drink, and if the competition lasts more than two hours, they can consume some glycogen gel for an energy boost.

Warm-Up

Jumpers should start their warm-up with a slow and easy jog for ten to fifteen minutes. The purpose of this is simply to raise the body temperature—a literal warm-up. After jogging, it is time to stretch.

Static Stretches

Shoulder and Triceps Stretch

- Stand tall, with your feet slightly wider than shoulder width apart and knees slightly bent.

- Place both hands above your head, and then slide both of your hands down the middle of your spine.

- You will feel the stretch in the shoulders and the triceps.

Hamstring Stretch

- Sit on the ground with both legs straight out in front of you.

- Bend the left leg, and place the sole of the left foot alongside the knee of the right leg.

- Allow the left leg to lie relaxed on the ground.

- Bend forward, keeping the back straight.

- You will feel the stretch in the hamstring of the right leg.

- Repeat with the other leg.

Hip and Thigh Stretch

- Stand tall with your feet approximately two shoulder widths apart.

"I usually aim for about 30 to 40 meters in my approach, which is about sixteen to eighteen steps. The most important thing is the last 10 meters coming off the board. That's not acceleration time. That's at top-end speed."

– Christian Taylor, two-time Olympic triple jump gold medalist

Stretching out the hips and thighs prepares the muscles high jumpers use for takeoff and twisting over the bar.

- Turn your feet, and face to the right.

- Bend your right leg so that the right thigh is parallel with the ground and the right lower leg is vertical.

- Gradually lower the body.

- Keep your back straight, and use your arms to balance.

- You will feel the stretch along the front of the left thigh and along the hamstrings of the right leg.

- Repeat by turning and facing to the left.

Adductor Stretch

- Stand tall with your feet approximately two shoulder widths apart.

- Bend your right leg and lower your body.

- Keep you back straight, and use your arms to balance.

- You will feel the stretch in the left leg **adductor**.

- Repeat with the left leg.

Groin Stretch

- Sit with a tall posture.

- Ease both of your feet up toward your body, and place the soles of your feet together, allowing your knees to come up and out to the side.

- Rest your hands on your lower legs or ankles, and ease both knees toward the ground.

- You will feel the stretch along the insides of your thighs and groin.

Dynamic Stretches

Arm Swings

- Stand tall, with your feet slightly more than shoulder width apart and knees slightly bent.

- Keep your back straight at all times.

- Swing both arms continuously to an overhead position and then forward, down, and backwards, with six to ten repetitions

- Swing both arms out to your sides, and then cross them in front of your chest, with six to ten repetitions

Leg Swings

- Stand sideways next to a wall with your weight on your left leg and your right hand on the wall for balance.

- Swing your right leg forward and backward, with six to ten repetitions on each leg.

66 The run-up is around twenty steps. The first steps are just to build the speed, and after you have to continue to accelerate. You have to think of a plane. Accelerate to takeoff. 99

— Damien Inocencio, Chinese national pole vault coach

Lunges With a Twist

- Stand tall with both feet together in the starting position.

- Keeping your back straight, lunge forward with the right leg.

- The right thigh should be parallel with the ground and perpendicular to your right lower leg.

- Slowly twist your torso at the waist toward the side you are lunging.

- Spring back to the starting position.

- Repeat with the left leg.

- Do six to ten repetitions on each leg.

Hip Stretch With a Twist

- Start in the push-up position, and bring your right foot up to your right hand while keeping your hips down and lower back flat.

- Lift your left hand, and twist to your left while extending your arm and reaching toward the sky.

- Come back to the starting push-up position, and repeat on the other side.

After stretching, it is time for jump-specific drills. Here are some examples:

Lunges are a good exercise for long jumpers, who need powerful thighs to increase jumping power.

- 5–10 x 50 meter or 5–10 x 100 meter sprints: These focus on correct running technique and maintaining a fast leg turnover. These should be done with rolling starts, where the jumper gradually picks up pace after slow jogging for the first ten meters. Each rep should be a little faster than the previous one, with the final one being at about 95 percent of top speed.

- Stationary pop-ups: These emphasize proper jump mechanics, where the jumper drives off the take-off leg, focusing on knee lift and a tall body position.

These dynamic movements speed up the muscle contraction rate to help maximize power and speed.

THROWING
Throwing includes the field events of shot put, discus, and javelin.

What to Wear
As with the jumping events, dress for the weather, and bring clothing to help stay warm between attempts.

What to Eat
As with the jumping events, athletes in the throwing events do not need to carb load on the day of a meet. The last full meal should be eaten between three and four hours prior to competition. A lean meat sandwich (e.g., turkey on whole grain bread) with fruit,

> 66 I practice running not for time because I can run relaxed when it's not timed. As soon as it is timed, I get really tight and try to run fast. So (training) isn't about times, it's about doing it correctly. 99

– Brianne Theisen-Eaton, world indoor champion, pentathlon

beans, and nuts is an example of a good meal option. This should be accompanied by sixteen to twenty ounces of whole chocolate milk. About an hour before competing, a small snack like a low-fat granola bar or a piece of fruit is a good idea. This can be accompanied by a protein shake. During the competition itself, athletes should focus on staying hydrated. Fluid intake will vary based on weather conditions as more will be required on hot days. In general, athletes should drink about eighteen ounces an hour. On hot days, they should include eight ounces of an electrolyte replacement drink as well. If the competition lasts more than two hours, they can consume some glycogen gel for an energy boost.

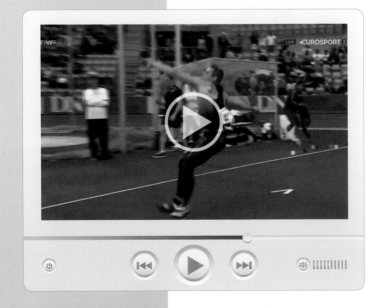

Watch Olympic javelin champion Thomas Röhler in Diamond League competition.

Warm-Up

Warming up for the throwing sports also focuses on increasing the force of muscle contractions and muscle contraction rates, but in throwers this is primarily in the upper rather than lower body. These events use a different set of muscle groups than jumpers and runners or use them in a different way.

Five to ten minutes of light jogging or, if available, riding a stationary bike will increase the body temperature, loosening the muscles. Stretching should then follow, using some of the lower body stretches outlined in the jumpers' section and mixing in some more upper body exercises.

> *If you start thinking about the line, you will break too early. You will lower your speed in the run-up. You will think about the line and want to stop, but javelin is all about one direction and full power.*
>
> *– Thomas Röhler, 2016 Olympic gold medalist*

Chest Stretch

- Stand tall, with your feet slightly wider than shoulder width and knees slightly bent.

- Hold your arms out to the side parallel with the ground with the palms of your hand facing forward.

- Stretch your arms as back as far as possible.

- You should feel the stretch across your chest.

Biceps Stretch

- Stand tall, with your feet slightly wider than shoulder width and knees slightly bent.

- Hold your arms out to the side parallel with the ground with the palms of your hand facing forward.

- Rotate your hands, so the palms face to the rear.

- Stretch your arms back as far as possible.

- You should feel the stretch across your chest and in the biceps.

Upper Back Stretch

- Stand tall, with your feet slightly wider than shoulder width and knees slightly bent.

- Interlock your fingers, and push your hands as far away from your chest as possible, allowing your upper back to relax.

- You should feel the stretch between your shoulder blades.

Shoulder Circles

- Stand tall, with your feet slightly wider than shoulder width and knees slightly bent.

- Raise your right shoulder toward your right ear, and move it backward, down, and then up again to the ear in a smooth action.

- Do six to ten repetitions.

- Repeat with the other shoulder.

"As you shift on to your left leg, it's going to basically set it up so you swing your right leg wide and kind of aggressively to create the momentum to pull you into the ring."

– Jared Schuurmans, 2015 U.S. national champion, discus throw

TEXT-DEPENDENT QUESTIONS:

1. What are the three basic types of events?

2. Why is carb loading unnecessary for sprinters?

3. How long prior to their event should throwing or jumping athletes eat their last full meal?

RESEARCH PROJECT:

Take some time, and put together a pre-event routine for yourself. Be detailed in each element, outlining specific numbers of repetitions for drills and so on. Be sure to be specific to your primary event. Outline meals, rest, and all the necessary components that you feel could help best prepare you before a big meet.

WORDS TO UNDERSTAND:

anxiety: fear or nervousness about what might happen

contradictions: things that are opposite or very different in meaning to something else

physiology: a branch of biology that deals with the processes and activities that keep living things alive

Chapter 2

THE RIGHT MIND-SET

Without proper mental preparation, it is very unlikely that an athlete will perform as well as possible. The world's best runners and field athletes now often see sports psychologists who can give them the mental edge that they need to succeed in training and competition.

Athletes need to make having a positive mental attitude a habit, but that takes training.

THINK POSITIVE

There are many reasons that some talented athletes become some of their sport's best, whereas others never see that talent fully realized. One of the most important is a positive frame of mind. Professionals are now taught techniques to keep a Positive Mental Attitude (P.M.A.) to improve their performance.

Acquiring a P.M.A. begins with learning how to control your thoughts. Say only positive things to yourself when you think about that long jump or race coming up. Instead of "I'll never win this event," tell yourself, "I can become a top competitor in this event." Instead of "That person is so much better than me," you must think, "I will learn everything I can from that person to improve my performance." When you catch yourself focusing on negative thoughts, immediately follow them up with positive **contradictions**. Repeat this pattern often enough, and you will find that P.M.A. becomes a habit—and you will find that competitors or difficult events will not so easily discourage you.

It takes training to make P.M.A. a habit. Just like you train your body, it is equally important to train your mind. Schedule specific time for mental training, creating positive visual pictures of your performance in running, throwing, or jumping events. The key is to imagine everything, down to the last detail. For example, picture yourself in the 1500 meter race pushing out ahead of the pack toward the finish line; hear the noise of the crowd cheering, and feel your shoes hitting the track and the sensation of your deep breathing. Mentally rehearse your technique until it is perfect. Also picture your tactics. In the 1500 meter, a common tactic is to run close behind another competitor to reduce wind resistance. Then, as you approach the finish line, use the energy you have conserved throughout the race to sprint ahead of the other runner and pass him or her across the finish line. Practice this tactic in your imagination, and visualize the success it brings you.

This tactic is called imagery, and athletes in many sports have embraced it as a way to have their minds help their bodies perform better. Research has shown that athletes who use imagery produce better race and event results than those who do not.

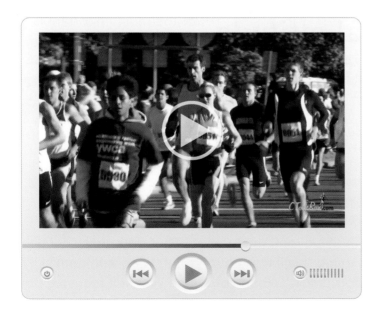

National Collegiate Athletic Association (NCAA) champion and 2004 Olympian Carrie Tollefson talks about mental preparation with Coach Dennis Barker.

P.M.A. comes not only from the way you think but also from how you carry yourself. To see what this means, try this experiment: stand up straight, pull back your shoulders, and lift up your chin. Put a big smile on your face, even if it feels artificial. Go for a brisk ten-minute walk, swinging your arms and filling your lungs with air. Use all your senses to enjoy the world around you. As you do this, you should begin to feel more energetic, lively, and less prone to depression or **anxiety**. The fact is that our thoughts often follow what our bodies are doing rather than the other way around. By moving in a way that demonstrates you are confident, you may actually become confident.

So do not just think that you are a winner. Act like you are a winner. Stand up tall and proud, and imitate the confident athletic behavior of successful professional athletes. Strange as it may seem, acting as if you are going to win your race will actually increase your likelihood of doing so.

BE WILLING TO WORK HARD

Lack of focus and lack of discipline are two things that lead to injuries and poor performance. Committing to work hard can help correct both these problems.

If you are not willing to commit to the work required to overcome these issues, you should

Athletes need to commit to putting in the hard work and training required for their event or else consider whether they have enough passion to continue competing in it.

consider whether your current sport is the right one for you. You should have a passion for the sport. If this is not the case, it is a good idea to try out another sport or activity to see where your true niche is. However, it may also be that you are simply burned out from too much practice. Boredom kills commitment quickly, so invest in making your sport as interesting as possible. Here are some tips:

- Find out everything you can about your sport—reading books, watching videos, and attending events.

- Talk with professional athletes. Many elite track-and-field competitors have their own Web sites with blogs or links to e-mail them. Share your problems and thoughts with them, and you might find that they have experienced the same issues in their training.

- Make the effort to travel to watch world-class athletes compete, and be inspired by their performance.

- Organize social outings with other athletes and team members— training should be fun, not just hard work.

- Focus all your energies on winning a particular medal or competition. Although winning is certainly not the most important part of any sport, it will help you become motivated and driven.

- Keep a training journal that records everything about each training session and competition as well as every bit of progress.

Use these tips as a starting point for you to find the motivation to fully commit to your sport. Think of other ways to feed both your imagination and your passion for the sport.

DON'T BE AFRAID

The primary reasons for fear in an athlete are lack of preparation and lack of confidence. Without these, athletes can be afraid of many things: failure, injury, embarrassment, or letting the team down. Fear is a dangerous feeling to take into track-and-field events. Fear can take away your ability to concentrate and to move with confidence. In events such as the pole vault, this can be dangerous. When the vaulter is ascending heights of up to 52 feet 6 inches (16 m) on the pole, there is a point that he or she is

*The pole vault requires concentration and confidence.
A lapse in either could be very dangerous.*

upside down and facing away from the landing mat; all the vaulter can see is the ground beneath. Any lapse in concentration at this point could result in a dangerous fall. It is no coincidence that most serious sporting injuries happen at competitions: the pressure of competition leads to an increase in fear and apprehension and therefore an increase in accidents.

The goal for an athlete should not be to eliminate fear, as this is unrealistic, but rather to control it. By controlling fear, you can channel that energy to help you perform better. In fact, if you aren't nervous, that's when you should be most worried! Nerves are a sign that you are passionate and truly care about what you are doing. By remembering the imagery technique discussed in this chapter, you can take your jitters and anxiety and create a stronger performance.

WORK AND DISCIPLINE

Talent is an important component in track and field. Some athletes are just naturally faster or able to jump higher than others. However, the hard fact

Putting in the work and having discipline during training is a key to success. Another helpful tip is for athletes to keep a training journal to track progress.

is that without work and discipline, the dreams of the most talented athletes will stay dreams instead of becoming reality. The trick is to work out a plan of action to take you step-by-step toward your goals. Do this by following these steps:

- Try to picture your end goal, such as winning the World Championship or a local title. Make this picture very clear. Be sure that it is what you really want.

- Working backward through time, think of every step you need to take to reach that final goal. For example, to win a regional title, you must first be selected for the team. To be selected, you must pass the team tryouts on a particular date. To pass the team tryouts, you must improve your qualifying performance in the long jump. Work backward in this way until you are at the present.

- What you have now is a breakdown of your major goals into small, manageable steps. Look at the first step on your list. Devote all your resources to achieving this goal. The important point is that for each step, you develop an action plan. In short, an action plan is what you will actually do to make the step happen. Work out the practical needs, and then most importantly, start them now. Beware of phrases like "I'll start this tomorrow." Once you have made the decision to achieve something, start working toward it today.

- Draw up an action plan for your training routine. At the beginning of each week, write down in a diary when you will train, what you will work on, and what you hope to achieve by the end of each session.

Planning and preparation are what separate winners from other competitors. Keep a training log of everything that happened during a particular training session or competition. The advantage of a well-kept training log is that you can see exactly what you need to work on. It can also reveal why you are suffering from certain injuries. You may notice, for example, that new shoulder pain you are experiencing only started since you began attempting a new technique in shot put. This will indicate that you need to alter your technique or strengthen your shoulder muscles.

GOOD LEADERSHIP

An important component in the development of any athlete is to have the leadership of someone knowledgeable who has his or her best interests at heart. There are literally thousands of track-and-field coaches in the United States. Picking out the professionals who are committed to their athletes from the less qualified can be difficult. Here are some signs that will help you tell the difference. A good coach will practice the following:

- Explain techniques clearly and simply

- Have approved coaching qualifications from a governing body such as USA Track & Field (USATF)

A good coach will reinforce positive messages while maintaining clear objectives during training.

- Make you feel good about yourself, and give you plenty of positive feedback

- Give you days off to rest your body and mind

- Have a clear structure and objective to every training session

- Understand the **physiology** of sports, and know how to handle injuries

- Make time for extra training in preparation for competitions

SIDEBAR
Legacy of a Legend

From 1949 to 1972, Bill Bowerman was the track-and-field coach at the University of Oregon, and over those twenty-four seasons, he forged one of the greatest legacies in the sport. His teams won four national titles and produced twenty-four individual NCAA champions, including Steve Prefontaine, and sixty-four All-Americans. Bowerman sent thirty-three athletes to the Olympics and coached thirteen world record holders.

Outside of his coaching accomplishments, Bowerman made several notable contributions to the sporting culture in America. During a trip to New Zealand in 1962, he noticed people jogging as a means to keep fit, something that was not happening in America. He introduced it to the people of Eugene (home of the University of Oregon) by starting a jogging club that would eventually become a model for fitness programs across the country.

In 1964, Bowerman and one of his former runners at Oregon named Phil Knight started a footwear distribution company called Blue Ribbon Sports. Knight ran the business with Bowerman as the head designer, dedicated to helping athletes perform better. In 1971, the name of the company was changed to Nike, Inc., which is now a $20 billion leader in the sports apparel and equipment industry.

MEETS

Mental training is important throughout the process of improving as an athlete, but when it is time to compete is when this training becomes most important. Many fine athletes have been defeated in races because a lack of confidence interferes with their physical ability. Competitions are undoubtedly nerve-wracking events, but there are several things you can do to help you harness your nervousness so that instead of holding back your body, it makes you run faster.

- Pack up everything you need for your event before you go to bed the night before. This means you will probably sleep better and also have a more restful morning on the day of the race.

- Eat properly throughout the day. Do not eat large, meaty meals because these will make you feel sluggish and lacking in energy, particularly if your event is in the afternoon, following lunch. Also, make sure you have a good, healthy breakfast: cereal, toast, orange juice, and fruit. Breakfast is the most important meal because your brain needs it to start the day sharp and continue clearly thinking throughout the morning.

- Warm up properly once you get to the place where the race or event is being held. Not only will this loosen up your body and prepare it for the race, but it will also help you focus your mind on what you need to do.

- Psych yourself up. Focus 100 percent on the race ahead of you. Find a place by yourself, where you can shut out other concerns and concentrate on the techniques needed to win. If you find it helps, play your favorite music on your MP3 player. Also, do not be intimidated by other competitors. Concentrate solely on getting from the starting line to the finish line in the fastest possible time, and forget about others' behavior.

- Learn from your losses. Defeats are not easy to accept, but you must learn to cope with them if you are going to improve. Do not allow yourself to feel depressed or overthink a bad performance. Quickly concentrate on why the race was a problem, and write down in your training log anything that occurs to you. Return to your training with renewed enthusiasm, determined to conquer your problems and smash your times in the next race in which you compete.

> " I give myself an hour, two hours tops, to be upset or angry about a bad race. I think about what went wrong and why it might have gone wrong, but I don't beat myself up about it. "
>
> – Steve Scott, former U.S. record holder in the mile

TRACK YOUR RESULTS

It is important for your confidence and mental training to consistently track your results. Keep an account of your times, competition performance, and medals to help you see how far you have come and also to identify those areas that need more work. The best way of keeping track is through a training log.

The training log is a record, either a written or an electronic file, used for recording day-to-day details about your athletic training. The following are the types of information you want to include in each entry:

- date

- time

- weather

- type of workout or run

- type of footwear worn

- times or measurements achieved

- warm-up and cooldown techniques used

- special training techniques

- notes about performance or injuries

TEXT-DEPENDENT QUESTIONS:

1. What does P.M.A. stand for?

2. Name some tips to make your sport as interesting as possible.

3. What are some signs that will help you tell the difference between a good and bad coach?

RESEARCH PROJECT:

Set up a training log that corresponds to your event. After three months, compare your results using different warm-up techniques, training at different times of the day, different shoes, and so on. Be sure to change only one variable at a time to assess its impact on your results.

WORDS TO UNDERSTAND:

physiques: the form or structure of a person's body; bodily makeup

plyometrics: training that involves sudden bursts of power

tendons: a tough cord or band of dense, white fibrous connective tissue that unites a muscle with some other part (as a bone) and transmits the force that the muscle exerts

Chapter 3

TRAINING FOR SUCCESS

Athletes can only perform at their best if they are in good physical condition. Track-and-field athletes need strength and endurance in varying degrees, depending on their particular event. Increased strength and flexibility in the vulnerable muscles, **tendons**, and ligaments surrounding the joints also helps to reduce the risk of injury. Athletes need to prepare the muscles and joints most at risk, those that endure repeated stress and heavy loads during exercise, or those that are exposed to sudden, explosive movements.

The triple jump is an example of an event that can result in overuse injuries in the muscles and tendons that join the thigh bone to the hip joint. By contrast, discus and javelin competitors are in danger of rupturing their back muscles from the twisting and hurling actions in their events.

PREPARING TO PREPARE

Before any workout or training exercise, it is crucial to warm up the body. Jumping right into an exercise is not smart, and more often than not, it will result in a sprained, torn, or otherwise injured body part. As tedious as it may seem, always take the proper time to warm up before practice or working out. Here are a variety of warm-up exercises that will get your blood pumping and muscles loosened no matter what your event.

Backward extension: Find a clear, open space with no obstacles, and begin running backward, extending your legs as far as they will reach. The goal is to get as much backward extension as possible to help develop fast-twitch muscles, hamstrings, quads, and hip flexors.

Jump skips for height: Skip on the right foot, and at the same time, drive your left knee up as high as it will go. Then repeat with the left foot skipping and the right knee driving up. The arms are very important in this drill as they must be constantly pumping up and down. Whichever foot is skipping on the ground, the same arm on the same side must be driving up as well.

Keep the arm at a ninety-degree angle from the elbows, with your hands pointed straight ahead and back and shoulders slightly arched. The goal is to obtain as much height as possible; this drill will develop proper form as you compete in an event.

Jump skips for distance: This is the same exercise as jump skips for height, but in this drill, focus on getting as far down the track as you can while extending the leg. Push off with the calf muscles and make sure your arms are driving up at a constant pace.

Karaoke: Standing up straight, look to the right over your shoulder, and put your hands out to the side for balance. Moving quickly but under control, cross your left leg over your right leg. Then, stride with your right leg toward the direction you are moving, and cross your left leg behind your right one, swiveling your hips as you move sideways. Continue this pattern quickly, crossing and uncrossing your legs as fast as you can. This exercise will increase your speed and reaction time.

Maximums: This drill is a great way to warm up as well as improve your running form. Start by running a 50-yard (46-meter) distance at about 50 percent (100 percent being a sprint as fast as you can possibly go.) Focus on keeping proper running form, drive your arms, relax your hands and jaw, and make sure your knees are driving up high and far, so you get as long a stride as possible. Stop at 50 yards (46 meters), walk back, and rest for one minute. Run the same distance again, but increase to 60 percent effort, then 70 percent, 80 percent, 90 percent, and finally 100 percent at a full sprint. At each speed, be sure to maintain proper form.

Stretching to help in warming up the muscles is essential before any training or exercise routine.

Watch former Big Ten 400 meter hurdles champion Jaret Campisi's training tips.

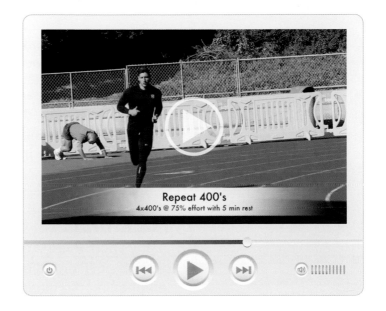

Repeat 400's
4x400's @ 75% effort with 5 min rest

PHYSICAL DURESS

Each type of event affects the body in a different way. Athletes must have well-rounded **physiques** that are strong and flexible at every level. However, they must also condition the parts of the body that are put under the most stress by their chosen events:

- running—hamstrings, quadriceps, ankles, foot flexors, and the gluteus maximus

- discus—shoulders, arms, lower back, hips, and knees

- javelin—shoulders, elbows, groin, upper and lower back, and hips

- hammer—shoulders, elbows, back, abdominals, hips, and knees

- shot put—shoulders, arms, abdominals, back, and legs

- high jump—spine, ankles, knees, and hips

- pole vault—shoulders, abdominals, and back

- long jump—ankles, knees, hips, and back

- triple jump—ankles, knees, hips, and back

The shot put causes stress on the shoulders, arms, abdominals, back, and legs.

Focusing on the muscle groups and joints that are most worked by their sport will improve performance and reduce the chance of injury for the athletes who compete in them.

FLEXIBILITY

In any sport, increased flexibility is a desired goal for athletes. This means lengthening the muscles to make them suppler. A flexible athlete has many advantages that a non-flexible athlete does not: a flexible muscle is far less likely to sustain injury under stress because it has a greater range of movement. Also, a flexible runner will be faster than one who is not flexible; he or she will be able to make longer strides with each step.

Stretching is the key to increasing flexibility. Regardless of the type of stretches, here are some general rules to follow:

- Stop immediately if you feel any sudden pains or growing burning sensations. Also, stop if you feel nauseated, faint, or ill in any way.

- Keep breathing deeply through any stretch—your muscles need a constant supply of oxygen to get the most out of the stretch.

- Make sure that you stretch both before and after a workout. The muscles, which will be tired and sore from being overworked, recover more quickly if they are stretched as the body is cooling down. Stretching prevents the muscles from tightening up and becoming stiff.

The following stretches are excellent for loosening up the hips, waist, and back—all areas that are prone to injury in track-and-field events.

Hip/Groin Stretch

- Stand with your legs in an A shape about two shoulder widths apart.

- Bend forward from the waist, and put your body weight on your hands.

- Slowly sink your hips downward, inching your legs wider and wider apart. Continue breathing deeply.

- When you are as far down as your body will allow, hold the position for five to ten seconds, and let your body relax. You may then be able to go down a bit farther.

- When you have reached your maximum stretch, come out of it by walking your feet inward (while maintaining your weight on your hands) until you are able to stand up.

Waist and Back Stretch

- Stand upright with your feet shoulder width apart.

- Bend straight forward from the waist, and lower your torso as far as it will go, keeping your back straight.

- Hold the legs, and gently pull on them to go down farther. Hold the stretch for ten seconds, then pull your body upright again.

- Put your hands against your lower back, and stretch your body backward, looking up at the ceiling as you do. Do not bend your head too far as this could lead to a neck strain. Hold for ten seconds.

Ankle Stretch

Sitting down, put your left ankle on top of your right knee. Hold the raised ankle with your left hand, and take hold of the toes and the ball of the foot with your right hand. Using your right hand, circle the foot around in one direction in large circles. Repeat about ten times, then reverse and repeat with the other foot.

Achilles Tendon Stretch

Lie on your back with both knees bent and feet flat on the floor. Straighten one leg up into the air, and hold it with both hands on the calf muscle. Pull your leg gently toward your face until it is at its maximum stretch. Then flex the raised foot slowly backward and forward about ten times, working the Achilles tendon.

Lower Leg Stretch

Sit on the floor with both legs straight out in front of you. Draw one leg in so that the sole of the foot sits against the inner thigh of the opposite leg. Sit up straight, and breathe in deeply, then exhale slowly, and bend forward from the hips and waist over the extended leg until you can grip your foot. Slowly pull on the toes so that the heel lifts slightly off the floor. You should feel a deep stretch along the back of the leg and knee. Lower the heel to the floor, and sit up slowly. Then reverse legs, and repeat the exercise.

> " I just pretty much feel what my body's trying to tell me, and I do a warm-up according to how that feels. Then I go into the call room and I start to visualize and focus on the execution of whatever event it is I'm doing that day. "
>
> – Tianna Bartoletta, two-time long jump world champion

Quadriceps Stretch

Stand up straight, resting one hand against a wall for stability. Lift your leg behind you, grasp the top of the foot with your left hand, then pull the heel up toward your buttocks. You should feel the stretch along the front of the thigh and knee. Hold the position for about thirty seconds, then let go of the foot, and return it to the floor. Repeat with your right leg.

TRAINING

Training for track and field includes many different aspects designed to build strength, power, and endurance. Not only must you practice your specific event, but it is also important to focus on separate areas and strengths of the body individually. For both field and running events, diverse training is essential. Strength and plyometric training are useful for field and sprinting events. For events that take place over a longer period of time, such as distance running, endurance is extremely important.

Exercises like this quadriceps stretch help promote flexibility in the legs.

SIDEBAR

Eat to Win

Follow this nutrition plan from some of the country's top nutritionists as a guide for eating effectively.

1. Eat Breakfast: Blood sugar is already low when you wake up, so instead of skipping breakfast, it should become a priority. A bagel with cream cheese or peanut butter along with yogurt and juice provides both carbs and protein.

2. Hydrate: Drink water throughout the day, not just during or after exercise. Try to drink about an ounce of water for every pound of body weight each day.

3. Stay Healthy: Food, as our main source of nutrients, is also our main source of immunity-boosting antioxidants and probiotics. Greek yogurt, colorful fruits and vegetables, and walnuts and flax seed should be staples in a diet that keeps you healthy on the inside.

4. Metal Servings: Iron deficiency is a problem many female athletes face. Low iron makes it more difficult for your blood to distribute oxygen effectively. Foods like spinach, red meat, cereal, and oatmeal will provide this essential element.

5. Have a Plan: To avoid getting caught having to order something less than optimal because you are pressed for time, plan ahead, and map out your meals a week at a time. Be sure to include healthy snacks in your plan.

6. Eat: Reducing your calorie intake sends your body the wrong signals and causes it to store calories instead of burning them. Eating the right foods regularly will make your body an efficient food processing machine.

7. Carbs Are Your Friend: This is true for any athlete. Carb loading right before an event is only useful if it tops up an already primed energy store. Be sure to include a steady amount of carbs in your everyday diet.

8. The Aftermath: Recovery is a key part of the nutrition process. A high-protein source like a whey protein shake immediately after exercise will aid recovery and lead to less muscle soreness.

Plyometrics

Certain field and sprinting events involve quick, explosive movements, the kind that are boosted by **plyometrics**. Plyometric training is a vital part of training in any sport that involves sudden bursts of power. A relatively modern branch of sports training, it aims to condition the muscles to make contraction movements in a short amount of time. Plyometric exercises have to be specifically tailored to the individual sport or event to be the most effective. For example, if you are a javelin or discus thrower, focus on upper-body plyometrics; if you do the long jump, lower-body plyometrics will help you the most.

The key characteristic of plyometric exercises is their stop-and-go nature. They focus on short, vigorous movements followed instantly by a relaxation phase. They are now an essential part of any field or sprint athlete's training regime because they are extremely useful in reducing injuries. But always be sure to learn these exercises under the supervision of a qualified coach or personal trainer. There are many plyometrics exercises, so your coach should be able to provide you with a practice routine specific to your event(s). Here are two basic exercises to demonstrate.

Exercises like this one, where the athlete jumps from the ground to the top of a wall or box, condition the legs for sprint starts and jumping events.

Upper Body

The athlete lies on the floor with a partner standing over him or her. The partner drops a medicine ball from a height at the chest of the athlete. The athlete catches the ball and immediately throws it back. This exercise trains the rapid expansion and contraction of the arms that is vital for throwing events.

Lower Body

The athlete jumps from the ground onto a box or step between twelve and thirty-one inches (thirty to eighty centimeters) high then immediately jumps back off. This should be practiced carefully, beginning with a lower height and working upward. It conditions the legs for spring starts and for jumping events.

Strength Training

The body uses its muscles to lift, pull, and push. The stronger the muscle, the more weight it can move. Strength training, or resistance exercises, are those that build muscle. They create stronger and larger muscles by producing more and tougher muscle fibers to cope with the increasing weight demands.

Weight training uses either free weights or weight machines to strengthen muscles. However it carries real risk of injury if done incorrectly, especially

Weight training builds muscle for greater strength and more durable muscle fiber.

for athletes who are under eighteen years old. Always get professional training first from your coach or other instructor before trying anything on your own. Follow these key rules for safe and effective results:

- When learning any new technique, practice it first without any weight at all until you can demonstrate perfect technique to an instructor. Once you have the right technique, add only light weights that you can handle easily.

- Add further weights in 1- to 3-pound (0.5–1.5-kilogram) increments, and perform one to three sets at the new weight. Once you can demonstrate perfect technique again at the new weight, more weight can continue to be added.

- Do not weight train more than three times a week in thirty-minute sessions.

- Do all exercises slowly, with total control and concentration. It should take three full seconds to perform the power phase of the exercise and three full seconds to relax the weight.

- Keep breathing deeply throughout the power phase and during the relaxation phase.

- Always warm up thoroughly before doing weights or any exercise. Cold muscles are susceptible to injury.

- Be systematic about how you develop your body. Always develop your muscles in antagonistic pairs. This means that if you develop, for example, the bicep on the inside of the arm, you should also work to develop the triceps on the outside of the arm equally. This concept also applies to the back and abdominals and the quadriceps and hamstrings.

- If you are under eighteen, do not attempt heavy dead-lift exercises. These put too much strain on the developing physique. Weight training is not recommended for growing muscles.

Athletes should concentrate on the weight training exercises that are specific to their event. To get the best results, work one-on-one with your coach or personal trainer, who can help you develop a routine tailored to your event.

Distance runners maximize their aerobic training to build up endurance.

Endurance

Aerobic training pushes the body to require increased amounts of oxygen to perform. The body gets this oxygen by raising the heart and breathing rates then sustaining both at the increased level. Aerobic exercise is vital both for increasing endurance and for injury prevention because it strengthens the heart muscles and lungs to cope with strenuous exercise. By gaining endurance, you will be able to run or perform for a longer period of time without becoming exhausted and out of breath. This will not only increase your performance times but also your health.

Track athletes obviously run all the time, so they do a lot of aerobic training as a natural part of their preparation. They should not, however, rely upon running alone. The best aerobic fitness comes from cross-training, which entails mixing different aerobic events in your training schedule. Use two or three different types of aerobic training to ensure that your cardiovascular system is strong and also to develop different muscle groups. An excellent combination would be running, swimming, and cycling: running and cycling improve lower limb flexibility and strength, whereas swimming enhances the shoulders, arms, back, and abdominals. One caution: even if you are extremely fit in one sport, do not jump into a different sport at the same speed. Different sports have different muscular demands, so give your body time to adjust to the new exercise. Also, make sure that you have at least two days a week of complete rest. Any less than that and you run a risk of injury through overtraining because your muscles will not have time to recover or strengthen.

Besides running, swimming, and cycling, there are several other ways to work your heart and lungs. Pick ones that you most enjoy, so training can be more enjoyable rather than an obligation.

- jumping rope

- playing basketball

- roller skating or roller blading

- dancing

- kayaking

- ice skating

TEXT-DEPENDENT QUESTIONS:

1. What is an example of an event that can result in overuse injuries in the muscles and tendons that join the thigh bone to the hip joint?

2. What is the key characteristic of plyometric exercises?

3. What kind of training pushes the body to require increased amounts of oxygen to perform?

RESEARCH PROJECT:

Look into what is required to put together an effective off-season training program. What types activities not related to your event are best to keep in shape? How might off-season training vary by event?

 ## WORDS TO UNDERSTAND:

acronym: a word formed from the initial letter or letters of each of the successive parts or major parts of a compound term; also an abbreviation (e.g., FBI) formed from initial letters

notorious: generally known and talked of, especially widely and unfavorably known

rotator cuff: a supporting and strengthening structure of the shoulder joint that is made up of the capsule of the shoulder joint blended with tendons and muscles as they pass to the capsule or across it to insert on the head of the humerus

Chapter 4

TAKING CARE OF THE BODY: INJURIES AND NUTRITION

Track-and-field injuries can either be sudden (acute), or gradual, resulting from wear and tear over a long period of time. It is important to know not only how to treat these injuries once they occur but how to prevent them from happening in the first place. In a sport like track and field, where each event is specialized, specific areas of the body need special attention.

P.R.I.C.E.

Not all injuries need professional treatment. Most are nonserious sprains and strains, and these may be treated in three stages. The first of these stages can be easily remembered by using the **acronym** P.R.I.C.E., which stands for protection, rest, ice, compression, and elevation.

Icing an injury right away helps to prevent swelling.

Protection
Stop and move to a place or position where you can take pressure off the injury as soon as you feel an injury or any unexplained pain.

Rest
Restrict any activities that affect the injury to a minimum, including everyday walking, for at least a week. Give the injured area complete rest.

Ice
Applying ice packs about two or three times a day, for no longer than twenty minutes each time, will reduce any swelling around the injury. If

there is no swelling, however, you may find it more helpful to apply heat treatments after the first few days. Heat-generating ointments are available from sports stores and drug stores and are useful for reducing pain caused by muscle strains. Do not use heat treatments on swollen areas.

Compression

Applying pressure around the injury reduces swelling and also protects the joint or muscle against further damage. Wrap the injury firmly in a bandage or athletic tape, or use a professional compression bandage.

Elevation

Elevating an injured leg above the level of the hips reduces the amount of blood flowing into the limb and helps reduce swelling.

Former National Association of Intercollegiate Athletics (NAIA) champion Scott Halley demonstrates how to prevent injury while throwing the javelin.

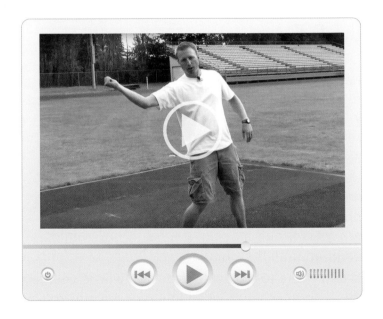

EVENT-SPECIFIC INJURIES

Because the sport of track and field can vary so much from event to event, you cannot always take training, warm-up, or injury-related advice from a teammate, especially if he or she competes in the long jump and you throw shot put. The descriptions listed here will show you what you need to watch out for during training and competition and how to best deal with injuries if they do occur. Again, always be sure to consult with your coach or trainer because he or she will ultimately know what is best for your situation.

Events like the discus put enormous pressure on the shoulder's rotator cuff.

Throwing Injuries

Throwing injuries mainly affect the upper limbs. Discus throwing, shot put, javelin, and hammer throw all have different actions, but all put immense strain on the shoulder's rotator cuff, the biceps and triceps in the arms, and the elbow. The elbow and shoulder often suffer the most injuries.

The arm's rotational movement around the shoulder joint is made possible by the rotator cuff, the group of muscles and tendons that attach the upper arm bone (the humerus) to the shoulder joint. The **rotator cuff** allows for more than 75 percent of all shoulder injuries in sports. Athletes throwing shot puts and hammers are particularly prone to rotator cuff injuries because of the weight of the object being thrown.

A torn rotator cuff means total rest from training. Reduce arm activity to a minimum until the pain in the shoulder has subsided, which may take about a week. Use the P.R.I.C.E. procedure, also, under the guidance of a doctor or pharmacist, and use anti-inflammatories to bring pain and swelling under control.

Moving the arm gently through its full range of movement (R.O.M. exercises) can be simple and effective. To strengthen the shoulder, try upper-arm weight training exercises using light 1-pound (500-gram) dumbbells. Vary the exercises frequently to strengthen all parts of the rotator cuff.

The javelin and discus are **notorious** for being tough on the elbow joint. When a thrower winds up for the throw, the throwing arm trails behind with the elbow locked under high g-forces. Then the elbow is whipped straight during the throw, particularly if the thrower's technique is poor. The classic injury to the elbow from field events is aptly called "thrower's elbow."

The first line of treatment for thrower's elbow and similar injuries is P.R.I.C.E., R.O.M., and strengthening exercises. Start R.O.M. exercises as soon as possible. The elbow has a tendency to stiffen up dramatically after injury and can degenerate further if the joint is not loosened.

 SIDEBAR

Common Track & Field Injuries

Repetitive stress injuries are the most common type in track and field. These are caused by overuse of a certain muscle or tendon to the point that it wears or breaks down. This is a gradual process that manifests itself over time, unlike an acute injury, like falling after crashing into a hurdle.

Trainers say there are two ways to reduce the chance of having a repetitive stress injury: use proper technique and stretch before and after exercising.

Runner's knee is caused by running out of balance, landing on the heels while running, and poor posture.

Jumper's knee, also known as patellar tendinitis, is caused by repeated stress on the patellar tendon in the joint while jumping. Stretching the quadriceps and hamstring properly before exercising can help to prevent it. Icing the knee can help to treat it.

Shin splints is the common name for soreness in the front of the leg, caused either by sore muscles or very small hairline fractures in the tibia. Flat feet or fallen arches can also lead to the development of this problem. Icing, anti-inflammatory medication, arch support shoe inserts, and rest are the best solutions.

RUNNING AND JUMPING INJURIES

The ankles, knees, hamstrings, and back are the areas most at risk of injury in running and jumping events. Ankles and knees suffer mainly from sudden thrusting forces as athletes begin a sprint and, for jumpers, when they push off violently for a jump. In the case of long jumpers and triple jumpers, the lower limbs also have to withstand impacts in the sand pit.

Torn muscles, tendons, and ligaments top the short list of common ankle injuries encountered in track and field. Ankle joints can develop a range of problems from jumping activities, the symptoms of which include reduced mobility, pain, difficulty in putting pressure on the joint, limping, and general discomfort. P.R.I.C.E. will control the swelling and pain of the injury. Like with the elbow, the ankle will benefit from early R.O.M., but keep this light to prevent overworking the already damaged joint.

The knee is very prone to injury in events like the long jump.

As with all the injuries described, stop rehabilitation exercises immediately if you have any sudden or increasing pains.

Minor knee injuries can usually be treated adequately using P.R.I.C.E., R.O.M., and strengthening exercises. You may benefit, however, from reducing the P.R.I.C.E. period or even skipping it altogether. Studies in knee rehabilitation have found that an injured knee joint tends to benefit from movement and light exercise. Sitting on a high chair or table, practice moving the lower leg backward and forward through its full range of movement to reintroduce mobility and strength. For additional support, you can put a physical therapy ball under the foot to take pressure off the knee. Further strengthening is available through lower limb weight-training exercises but only if you experience no significant pain. Try the exercises without weights before proceeding.

For the first few weeks, ease back to running gradually, and try to avoid running continuously around track bends—these put the knee under more pressure. Consult a doctor if the pain in the knee increases or knee flexibility decreases at

Hamstring injuries are common in running and jumping events like the hurdles.

any time during rehabilitation. Also consult a doctor if the joint feels unstable or its movement is rough.

The hamstrings are commonly damaged in running and jumping events. They are a group of three muscles set at the back of each thigh that flex the knee joint. They are usually damaged in sprinting, especially during explosive starts from the blocks and fast accelerations. The injured person may feel a distinctive popping sensation at the moment of rupture, followed by pain at the back of the thigh and limited mobility in the knee. Sometimes, there may be swelling and even bruising behind the knee. Most hamstring injuries are fully treatable by following the P.R.I.C.E., R.O.M., and strengthening procedures.

The back undergoes extreme twisting forces during field events, putting both jumping and throwing competitors at risk for back injuries. Muscles are easily ruptured, and even the spine itself can be damaged. A doctor should always be seen for back injuries because some can be very serious.

Pulled back muscles are common in throwing and jumping events. Its main symptom is severe pain in the lower back, made worse through movement or lifting. Treat initially with complete rest, lying down as much as possible on a firm, supportive surface. Drawing your knees up with the feet flat on the surface will ease the pain by pushing the small of the back down onto the bed for support. As the pain diminishes, introduce light exercise to increase flexibility and strength.

NUTRITION AND SUPPLEMENTS

Practice, preparation, and training are to important parts of being safe and successful in track and field. You also need to think about what you take into your body. What you eat, and when you eat it, is just as important as training and exercise. An improperly fueled body cannot perform at an optimal level. Eating the right things is obviously essential, but it is not quite that simple. Quantity of nutrients and when they are consumed are also key factors in developing a good nutrition program. It is not recommended that athletes develop these programs on their own. A professional dietician, nutritionist, or physician should be consulted in putting together the proper plan tailored to individual athletes.

> *Don't change anything in the last few days before a race. Stick to the safe, boring food that you've been using in training. Stick to the same drinks and the same race day breakfast you've been having in your training runs.*
>
> *– Paula Radcliffe, women's marathon world record holder*

WHAT TO EAT

Although a balanced diet is important for everyone, it is even more important for athletes. Typically an athlete has to eat considerably more than other people do. The United States Food and Drug Administration (FDA) suggests that the average American should eat about 2,000 calories a day; for a male high school- or college-level athlete, a 3,000- to 4,000-calorie diet is more common. There are three main food groups to consider when choosing a diet: carbohydrates, protein, and fats.

Carbohydrates

Carbohydrates are foods rich in a chemical called starch, which is what the body breaks down to get energy. Starchy foods include breads and grains, vegetables such as potatoes, cereal, pasta, and rice. There is no one-size-fits-all formula that can exactly dictate what an athlete's carb consumption should be. A general rule is that in season or during times of intense training, athletes should eat about 5 grams (0.2 ounces) of carbs for every

Good sources of carbohydrates include grains, bread, potatoes, and pasta.

pound (0.5 kilogram) of body weight. In the off-season or during periods of lower training levels, it should be about 2 to 3 grams (0.07–0.10 ounces) per pound. The body uses carbs strictly for fuel, so if they are not being burned, they are turned into fat and stored. Therefore it is important to adjust carb intake based on activity level. Athletes should not eat heavily processed carbohydrates such as white sugar and white flour. These simple carbs are quickly broken down into sugars, which the body processes into fats if it does not immediately burn them off. The best carbohydrate choices for an athlete are complex types like pasta and whole-grain foods as well as starchy vegetables. A nutritious diet avoids empty calories or those provided by food that lacks other nourishment, like processed sugar and starches.

Protein

Unlike carbohydrates, protein is used within the body. Proteins are important chemicals used to perform specific functions inside our body's cells. Our bodies can break down proteins that are found in foods and use them to build new proteins that make up our muscles and bones. During periods of intense training and activity, the body needs more protein to repair damage to muscles. Not eating enough protein can cause an athlete to lose muscle mass and negatively affect the ability to perform. The Academy of Nutrition and Dietetics recommends athletes consume about 0.50 to 0.75 gram (0.02–0.03 ounce) of protein for every pound (0.5 kilogram) of body weight. During the season or heavy training, that number should be closer to a full gram (0.04 ounces) per pound. This higher ratio is also true if an athlete is trying to build muscle mass. The best sources of proteins are lean meats and dairy products (such as milk or cheese) as well as eggs and certain types of soy, beans, and nuts.

Fats

Lots of times, we think of fats as bad for us because eating too much of them is unhealthy. However, fat is an important ingredient needed to make our bodies work correctly. They help balance hormone production, support cell growth and protect our organs, among other functions. Without fat, our bodies cannot absorb certain vitamins as well as they should. Also, our skin and hair need some amount of fat to grow correctly. However, fat should still be eaten in moderation as it is higher in calories than protein or carbs. No more than 70 grams (2.5 ounces) a day is recommended. All fats are not created equal, however. Trans fats and saturated fats found in processed foods are

Fats like those found in olive oil and nuts are healthy but should be limited to 70 grams (2.5 ounces) per day.

high in bad cholesterol, which clogs arteries and is bad for the heart. The best sources of fat are vegetable oils, olive oil, and nuts.

DIETARY SUPPLEMENTS

Ideally, a balanced diet would provide our bodies with all the nutrients it needs. However, due to many varying factors, eating optimally is not always possible. Dietary supplements are available to fill dietary gaps created by a deficient diet.

In discussing dietary supplements here, this does not include banned performance-enhancing substances. Instead, the focus here is on supplements that contain vitamins, minerals, and other compounds that help the body absorb nutrients or recover more efficiently. When properly used supplements can improve overall health and performance, but you should always consult a doctor or other expert before using them to augment your diet or training program. Some examples of common supplements include vitamin tablets and protein shakes or powder.

Vitamin Tablets

For many reasons, we do not always get the vitamins and nutrients we need. Often, this is because our diets are not as balanced as they should be. Sometimes, it is because the foods that are available to us have been processed in such a way that they lose nutrients. If you know or suspect that a certain key vitamin is underrepresented in what you are eating, in many cases, the necessary vitamins can be obtained from vitamin supplements. These supplements, which are usually taken as a pill, can either contain a balanced mixture of vitamins and nutrients (multivitamins) or contain a single vitamin or mineral that our diet is lacking. The best way to avoid this issue is to work hard to eat right whenever possible.

Protein Supplements

Getting enough protein from the food you eat can be difficult as well. For athletes, eating protein immediately after a workout is recommended (to

Protein shakes are an effective way to supplement the diet when there is no time to eat a balanced meal instead.

refuel the body), but most people either don't feel up to or do not have the time to spend cooking or preparing themselves a meal immediately after a workout. That is where protein shakes come in handy. These are a protein supplement sold in powder form that look and taste like milkshakes when blended with water but contain no dairy products. Protein shakes deliver a high ratio of protein to carbohydrates and calories. They are not meant to replace meals. Many other necessary nutrients are gained from a balanced diet that cannot be replaced by protein shakes, regardless of how fortified they may be.

Staying Hydrated

The body needs water more than it needs any other nutrient. If you are not getting enough water, your performance will suffer in spite of any preparation or balanced diet. Dehydration occurs when your body doesn't have enough water. Symptoms include fatigue, dizziness, and headaches. No athlete can perform at his or her best if not properly hydrated. Proper hydration should be maintained not only at meets but throughout training as well. The body does not store water, so we need to constantly maintain its supply. The American College of Sports Medicine recommends these guidelines for athletes:

- **Before Exercise:** Drink 16 to 20 ounces (473–591 milliliters) within the two-hour period prior to exercise.

- **During Exercise:** Drink 4 to 8 ounces (118–237 milliliters) every fifteen to twenty minutes during exercise.

- **Post Exercise:** Replace 24 ounces (710 milliliters) for every pound (0.5 kilogram) of body weight lost during exercise.

Staying fully hydrated can help concentration, improve digestive health, and reduce the risk of kidney stones.

TEXT-DEPENDENT QUESTIONS:

1. What kinds of injuries mainly affect the upper limbs?

2. Name three of the most common ankle injuries encountered in track and field.

3. Why don't we always get the vitamins and nutrients we need?

RESEARCH PROJECT:

Put together a sample nutrition plan for yourself by mapping out meals and snacks for a given week. Pick a week when you are training and competing. Be sure to consider the nutrition benefits of everything you choose as well as the time it will take to make the plan work in your busy schedule.

 ## WORDS TO UNDERSTAND:

amateur: one who engages in a pursuit, study, science, or sport as a pastime rather than as a profession

emergence: the act of becoming known or coming into view

staunch: steadfast in loyalty or principle

Chapter 5

TRACK AND FIELD: FROM MARATHON TO THE MODERN OLYMPICS AND MEASURING THE FUTURE

ANCIENT PEOPLE TO ANCIENT GREECE

Humans have been running, jumping, and throwing for as long as we have been on this planet. For early people, these activities were for survival, not sport. Running and throwing were primary defense tactics when faced with threats from predators. These skills evolved into ones of offense used in hunting animals for food and are the basis of modern-day events such as sprinting, javelin, shot put, and discus.

Hunting skills eventually became fighting skills as tribes settled into more permanent and stationary communities that had to be defended against hostile neighbors. Warriors were the athletes of the time. They were admired by the rest of the tribe and often given the best shelter and food. Eventually competition developed among warriors in tribes, leading to contests of skill or speed. These contests took place at festivals and funerals, and in ancient Greece, they led to the greatest sporting spectacle of all.

The Greeks have been competing at track and field for centuries, as depicted in this Roman copy of the ancient Greek statue by Myron called the Discobulus.

The Greeks are the best-known organizers of speed and skill contests. Evidence from 3,000 years ago shows that they competed in everything from javelin and discus throwing, distance running, and broad jumping to wrestling, archery, and chariot racing. Competitions featuring these and other events became prevalent in different areas of Greece at different times throughout each year. This continued for centuries, and one location that developed into a famous competition site known across the ancient world was at the city of Olympia.

Olympia at the time was famous throughout Greece as a shrine to Zeus, the Greek god of thunder. The earliest written records of the games held here in his honor are from 776 B.C., but there is evidence that the games at Olympia were ongoing for centuries prior to this date. They continued for several centuries more, contested every four years, and the growth in popularity of the games led to the construction of stadiums and eventually housing for the athletes as well. The games at Olympia became the most prestigious in all of Greece, and victory at these Olympic games gave its champions instant popularity and recognition, which in turn yielded invitations to other major events across the empire.

Chariot races provided the biggest spectacle at the Olympic Games, but the most popular athletes of the games competed in the pentathlon, a competition comprised of five events: discus throw, javelin throw, standing broad jump, 200 meter sprint, and a wrestling match. All but the wrestling match are current track-and-field events, with the standing broad jump having evolved into the modern long jump.

In ancient Greek (and other ancient patriarchal societies), women were not permitted to take part in anything deemed prestigious or important. This, of course, included the Olympic Games. The desire to compete burned bright in women even thousands of years ago, and many would disguise themselves as men just so they could take part in the games. Therefore, it became the rule that competitors in the Olympic Games were required to be naked. Not to be outdone, women began disguising themselves as male trainers, so they could watch. The rule then became that trainers also had to work naked.

Olympia fell to the Romans around 85 B.C., but the games continued under Roman rule for another 400 years. In 391 A.D., the emperor Theodosius I issued an edict closing all pagan temples, which led to the decline of the ancient Greek faith and many aspects of the ancient way of life, including the Olympics. The games at Olympia were gone by the fifth century. Historians believe the last of the buildings used for the Olympics were destroyed by earthquakes in the sixth century.

THE MARATHON AND THE MODERN OLYMPICS

One of the most well-known running events is the marathon, a long-distance race that tests the will and endurance of competitors. The marathon stems from the ancient story of Pheidippides. Pheidippides was a courier whose last and most famous assignment was to proclaim the Greek victory over the Persians at the Battle of Marathon in 490 B.C. According to the legend, Pheidippides ran 42 km (26.2 miles) from Marathon to Athens to deliver the message of triumph and then dropped dead immediately afterward. Although the race is based on the story of this event that took place at the height of the ancient Olympics, the Greeks did not come up with the idea of having a race synonymous with literally killing the competitors. That idea came from a Frenchman some 2,400 years later.

Pierre de Coubertin was an educator from Paris. He became a staunch advocate for teaching physical education in schools during a trip to observe schools in England in 1886. He saw the benefits to the English students, benefits that were lacking in France, where he tried but failed to gain support to introduce physical education. He then decided to think bigger.

In the early 1880s, de Coubertin traveled to Greece to visit the archeological digs at Olympia, where the buried Olympic buildings were being unearthed. When

The legend of the run of Pheidippides from Marathon to Athens in 490 B.C. inspired the original Olympic marathon in 1896. Uganda's Stephen Kiprotich won the 2012 version.

Pierre de Coubertin's visit to the archaeological dig at Olympia inspired him to revive the Olympic Games.

his physical education initiatives failed, he gained inspiration from his memories of Olympia and decided to try and revive the Olympic Games. By 1894, de Coubertin had managed to arrange a congress, held in Paris, on amateur sports. Out of these meetings came approval for an Olympic Games revival to be held every four years starting in 1896 at Athens. Events were to include cycling, sailing, gymnastics, wrestling, fencing, shooting, swimming, tennis, weightlifting, and athletics (the international name for track and field).

Fourteen countries sent teams to compete in Athens, including a ten-person team from the United States. Track and field contested twelve events: high jump, pole vault, long jump, triple jump, shot put, discus, 100 meter, 400 meter, 800 meter, 1500 meter, 100 meter hurdles and de Coubertin's invention, the marathon. The United States contingent did very well, winning nine of the twelve events, including double golds in the sprint events (Thomas Burke), throwing events (Robert Garrett), and jumping events (Ellery Clark). The marathon winner, however, was fittingly from Greece.

Spyridon Louis, a twenty-three-year old from nearby Marousi, won the race in 2:58:50, over the same route Pheidippides ran from Marathon to Athens. Legends of the race details abound. One story has Louis stopping at an inn in Pikermi (about halfway into the race) for a glass of cognac with his soon-to-be father-in-law. When told other runners had passed him, Louis was confident in his chances of recovering his advantage. Both the French and Australian runners ahead of him when he resumed were too overcome with exhaustion to finish the race. Louis entered the stadium in Athens to a thunderous hero's welcome, and reports say two of Greece's crown princes ran the final lap with him.

The marathon has been an event in every Olympic games, but Greece has never won a medal since 1896. It is not the marquee event now that it was then, however. The influence of television and the more spectator-friendly qualities of stadium events have made the sprints the feature events of any track-and-field competition, headlined by the 100 meter dash.

The great Carl Lewis is the only American man to win multiple gold medals in the 100 meter since 1968.

The first 100 meter Olympic champion was American Thomas Burke. The first women's race was held at the Amsterdam games in 1928 and won by American Betty Robinson. It is an event that Americans dominated in the early years of Olympic track and field. American men won twelve of the first sixteen 100 meter Olympic events from 1896 to 1968. Perhaps the most famous of these wins was by Alabaman Jesse Owens. Owens, an African American sprinting star at Ohio State, won three individual gold medals in each of the 100 meter, 200 meter, and long jump events. This was at the 1936 Berlin games in Adolf Hitler's Nazi Germany. Hitler had hoped these games would be a showcase for what he believed was the superiority of the white master race. Hitler watched as Owen's proved him wrong in front of the world.

American women won five of the first nine 100 meter Olympic events, including back-to-back wins for Wyomia Tyus in 1964 and 1968. Tyus, a Georgia native who ran track at Tennessee State, was the first person to successfully defend the Olympic 100 meter title.

Asafa Powell was the last man to hold the 100 meter world record before it was broken by his countryman Usain Bolt in 2008.

Since 1968, only three American men and three American women have won gold in the 100 meter, now track and field's premier event: Carl Lewis (twice), Maurice Greene, Justin Gatlin, Evelyn Ashford, Florence Griffith-Joyner, and Gail Devers (twice). Other nations have made great strides in the sprinting events, primarily the tiny island nation of Jamaica. The country of just 3 million people has produced some of the world's most prolific sprinters, and Jamaicans have won the last three Olympic 100 meter events for both men and women. This includes wins by Shelly-Anne Fraser in 2008 and 2012 and Elaine Thompson in 2016 for the women and three consecutive wins for Usain Bolt.

LIGHTNING BOLT AND DIAMOND LEAGUE

Thirty-two American men, including all of Owens, Lewis, Greene, and Gatlin, have held the world record, and the unofficial title of world's fastest man, in the men's 100 meter event. Jamaicans, however, have held the record since Asafa Powell broke Gatlin's record when Powell ran 9.76 seconds in 2006. The incomparable Bolt then broke that record in Beijing before setting the current mark of 9.58 seconds in 2009.

> *Worrying gets you nowhere. If you turn up worrying about how you're going to perform, you've already lost. Train hard, turn up, run your best and the rest will take care of itself.*
>
> *– Usain Bolt, nine-time Olympic champion*

Bolt's Olympic results in those 2008 Beijing games were unprecedented and spectacular. Not only did he set the world record in the 100 meter (9.69 seconds), but Bolt also broke the 200 meter world record as well (19.3 seconds), becoming the first man ever to break both records at the same Olympics.

Bolt's **emergence** was a shot in the arm for the sport of track and field, which has too often been plagued by doping scandals. Since the turn of the century, athletes like Gatlin and Americans Marion Jones and Tim Montgomery all had records or medals stripped due to failing drug tests. Many experts believe several women's world records from the 1980s are tainted as they were set by athletes from countries later shown to have promoted the use of performance-enhancing drugs in their athletic programs. Drugs and cheating had tainted the reputation of the sport, so track and field needed Usain Bolt.

Check out Usain Bolt's highlights from the 2016 Olympics.

After the Beijing Olympics, Bolt had a meteoric rise to international superstardom. He went on to win both the 100 meter and 200 meter events at both of the next two Olympic Games, a triple double that may well never be duplicated. Along the way, he also won an unmatched four consecutive

World Championship gold medals in the 200 meter. He would likely have done the same in the 100 meter were it not for a false start disqualification in the event at the 2011 World Championships.

Bolt is the unparalleled star of world athletics. With a personality every bit as big as his talent, Bolt is a media magnet, and fans flock to see him race. He is one of the best-known athletes in the world in any sport. Meet organizers happily pay his $250,000 appearance fee because they know it makes sponsors happy to have Bolt there and guarantees a sellout crowd. Bolt announced his retirement from Olympic competition following the 2016 games.

SIDEBAR
Andre De Grasse

The future of men's sprinting may have been announced at the 2016 Rio Olympics. At those games, twenty-one-year-old Andre De Grasse of Canada won one silver and two bronze medals, finishing behind Jamaica's Usain Bolt three times, including a relay race. The Toronto native was named the IAAF Rising Star for 2016 as a result.

De Grasse announced himself on the international scene in 2015 when he ran 9.92 seconds to claim bronze at the 2015 World Championships in Beijing. Four months after that showing, De Grasse turned pro. His success in 2016 garnered him recognition from his country, where he was named Canadian Male Athlete of the Year— and from Bolt himself.

"He's going to be good, he runs just like me," Bolt said after the 100 meter final in Rio.

"He feels like I'm the next one," De Grasse said of Bolt. "I'm just trying to live up to it."

What the International Association of Athletics Federation (IAAF) does when Bolt leaves the sport for good will be interesting to see. Track and field's governing body has already begun looking to the future, including recently revamping its Diamond League, a series of sixteen events for both men and women competed over fourteen international meets. The first twelve meets now serve as qualifiers for the two final championship meets. Previously, champions were determined by points earned over each of the fourteen meets, and titles could be determined in advance of the final meets. This move now gives the series a seasonal narrative.

In 2017, IAAF president Sebastian Coe also launched the Athletics Integrity Unit, an independent group tasked with overseeing track and field's anti-doping program. Drug cheating scandals have

World record holder Usain Bolt of Jamaica cruises to the win in the 100 meter final at 2009 meet in Greece.

marred the sport for decades. Examples range from entire federations sanctioning cheating, like East Germany in the 1980s and Russia in the 2010s, to famous gold medal winners being disgraced and stripped of their victories, from Ben Johnson to Marion Jones.

Will this be enough? Stars are the driving force behind track and field, like in many other sports, and fans want to know that the stars are playing clean. Stars want to know that making the trip to these Diamond League meets is worth their while, but the top prize for each event is just $50,000, or slightly more than $3,500 per meet. That is not much in terms of incentive for the top athletes. Bolt picked and chose which Diamond League events to compete at, never concerned with winning the title. He only won the 100 meter title once in eight seasons. He never won the 200 meter title.

Stars in other events have been more reliable at Diamond League meets. In the pole vault, world record holder Renaud Lavillenie of France has won the Diamond League title every year of its existence. U.S. 400 meter hurdler Kerron Clement was both the 2016 Olympic and Diamond League champion. Other top stars like David Rudisha and Christian Taylor are also regulars. For the women, Jamaica's Elaine Thompson was Olympic and Diamond League champion in the 100 meter in 2016. Other sprint stars like American Allyson Felix and Dafne Schippers of the Netherlands, hurdler Kendra Harrison, discus thrower Sandra Perković, and triple jumper Caterine Ibargüen are also Diamond League champions.

Jamaica's Elaine Thompson receives her gold medal for her victory in the 200 meter sprint at the 2016 Olympics.

Another draw for fans is the possibility of seeing a world record performance. In 2016, both Harrison (100 meter hurdles) of the United States and Bahrain's Ruth Jebet (3000 meter steeplechase) set world records at Diamond League meets. Both athletes are under twenty-five, and the world may not have seen the best from them yet. On the men's side, however, no world records occurred at Diamond League meets in 2016. In fact, Wayde van Niekerk was the only man to set a world record in 2016 and also compete in a Diamond League event. His world record in the 400 meters came at the Rio Olympics. Van Niekerk has the speed and talent of a star but competed in only two Diamond League 400 meter events in 2016, winning both. The stars get their money from sponsors, not relying on event purses for income. That is why appearance fees are paid to the top athletes by some meet organizers. With Bolt gone from the sport, it remains to be seen which current or future stars will be commanding those fees to keep stadium seats filled.

TEXT-DEPENDENT QUESTIONS:

1. What is one of the most well-known running events in which a long-distance race tests the will and endurance of competitors?

2. How many American men have held the world record and the unofficial title of world's fastest man in the men's 100 meter event?

3. In 2017, IAAF president Sebastian Coe launched what independent group tasked with overseeing track and field's anti-doping program?

RESEARCH PROJECT:

The United States has a rich and successful track-and-field history. In terms of Olympic and World Championship medals, what are three other successful countries in the sport, and what events and athletes have driven their success? Report on if and how the use of banned substances factors into the reputation of any of these countries, including the United States.

SERIES GLOSSARY OF KEY TERMS

Acute Injury: Usually the result of a specific impact or traumatic event that occurs in one specific area of the body, such as a muscle, bone, or joint.

Calories: units of heat used to indicate the amount of energy that foods will produce in the human body.

Carbohydrates: substances found in certain foods (such as bread, rice, and potatoes) that provide the body with heat and energy and are made of carbon, hydrogen, and oxygen.

Cardiovascular: of or relating to the heart and blood vessels.

Concussion: a stunning, damaging, or shattering effect from a hard blow—especially a jarring injury of the brain resulting in a disturbance of cerebral function.

Confidence: faith in oneself and one's abilities without any suggestion of conceit or arrogance.

Cooldown: easy exercise, done after more intense activity, to allow the body to gradually transition to a resting or near-resting state.

Dietary Supplements: products taken orally that contain one or more ingredient (such as vitamins or amino acids) that are intended to supplement one's diet and are not considered food.

Dynamic: having active strength of body or mind.

Electrolytes: substances (such as sodium or calcium) that are ions in the body regulating the flow of nutrients into and waste products out of cells.

Flexible: applies to something that can be readily bent, twisted, or folded without any sign of injury.

Hamstrings: any of three muscles at the back of the thigh that function to flex and rotate the leg and extend the thigh.

Hydration: to supply with ample fluid or moisture.

Imagery: mental images, the products of imagination.

Mind-Set: a mental attitude or inclination.

Overuse Injury: an injury that is most likely to occur to the ankles, knees, hands, and wrists, due to the excessive use of these body parts during exercise and athletics.

Plyometrics: also known as "jump training" or "plyos," exercises in which muscles exert maximum force in short intervals of time, with the goal of increasing power (speed and strength).

Positive Mental Attitude (P.M.A.): the philosophy that having an optimistic disposition in every situation in one's life attracts positive changes and increases achievement.

Protein: a nutrient found in food (as in meat, milk, eggs, and beans) that is made up of many amino acids joined together, is a necessary part of the diet, and is essential for normal cell structure and function.

Quadriceps: the greater extensor muscle of the front of the thigh that is divided into four parts.

Recovery: the act or process of becoming healthy after an illness or injury.

Resistance: relating to exercise, involving pushing against a source of resistance (such as a weight) to increase strength. Strength training, or resistance exercises, are those that build muscle. They create stronger and larger muscles by producing more and tougher muscle fibers to cope with the increasing weight demands.

Strategy: a careful plan or method.

Stretching: to extend one's body or limbs from a cramped, stooping, or relaxed position.

Tactics: actions or methods that are planned and used to achieve a particular goal.

Tendon: a tough piece of tissue in the body that connects a muscle to a bone.

Training: the process by which an athlete prepares for competition by exercising, practicing, and so on.

Warm-Up: exercise or practice especially before a game or contest—broadly, to get ready.

Workout: a practice or exercise to test or improve one's fitness for athletic competition, ability, or performance.

FURTHER READING:

Hollobaugh, J. *The 100 Greatest Track & Field Battles of the 20th Century.* CreateSpace Independent Publishing Platform, 2012

Schaap, Jeremy. *Triumph: The Untold Story of Jesse Owens and Hitler's Olympics.* New York, NY: Mariner Books, 2008

Stanbrough, Marck. *Motivational Moments in 2012 Olympic Track and Field (Motivational Moments in Track and Field).* Emporia, KS: Roho Publishing, 2013

INTERNET RESOURCES:

International Association of Athletics Federation: *http://www.iaaf.org/home*

USA Track & Field: *http://www.usatf.org/Home.aspx*

Olympic Athletics: *http://www.olympic.org/athletics*

FDA: Dietary Supplements: *http://www.fda.gov/Food/DietarySupplements/default.htm*

VIDEO CREDITS:

Watch Olympic javelin champion Thomas Röhler in Diamond League competition: *http://x-qr.net/1EqY*

NCAA champion and 2004 Olympian Carrie Tollefson talks about mental preparation with Coach Dennis Barker: *http://x-qr.net/1DN5*

Watch former Big Ten 400 meter hurdles champion Jaret Campisi's training tips: *http://x-qr.net/1DJS*

Former NAIA champion Scott Halley demonstrates how to prevent injury while throwing the javelin: *http://x-qr.net/1GqM*

Check out Usain Bolt's highlights from the 2016 Olympics: *http://x-qr.net/1DrE*

PICTURE CREDITS

QR CODES AND LINKS TO THIRD-PARTY CONTENT

INDEX

In this index, page numbers in **bold italics** font indicate photos or videos.

ABOUT THE AUTHOR

Peter Douglas is a former journalist, reporting on both sports and general news for many years at television stations in various locations across the US affiliated with NBC, CBS and Fox. Prior to his journalism career he worked with the Boston Red Sox Major League baseball team. An avid writer and sports enthusiast, he has authored 16 additional books on sports topics. In his downtime Peter enjoys family time with his wife and two young children and attending hockey and baseball games in his home city.